ZOMBIES

AMY HAYES

Cavendish
Square

New York

CREATURES OF FANTASY

ZOMBIES

BY

AMY HAYES

CAVENDISH SQUARE PUBLISHING · NEW YORK

Published in 2016 by Cavendish Square Publishing, LLC
243 5th Avenue, Suite 136, New York, NY 10016

Copyright © 2016 by Cavendish Square Publishing, LLC

First Edition

CPSIA Compliance Information: Batch #CW16CSQ

All websites were available and accurate when this book was sent to press.

Library of Congress Cataloging-in-Publication Data

Hayes, Amy.
Zombies / Amy Hayes.
pages cm. — (Creatures of fantasy)
Includes bibliographical references and index.
ISBN 978-1-5026-0926-7 (hardcover) ISBN 978-1-5026-0927-4 (ebook)
1. Zombies—Juvenile literature. I. Title.
GR581.H39 2016
398.21—dc23
2015029486

Editorial Director: David McNamara
Editor: Kristen Susienka
Copy Editor: Nathan Heidelberger
Art Director: Jeffrey Talbot
Designer: Joseph Macri
Senior Production Manager: Jennifer Ryder-Talbot
Production Editor: Renni Johnson
Photo Research: J8 Media

The photographs in this book are used by permission and through the courtesy of: Kiselev Andrey Valerevich/Shutterstock.com, cover; Jeff Thrower/ Shutterstock.com, 2-3; Alexander Tihonov/Shutterstock.com, 6; Christian Aslund/Lonely Planet Images/Getty Images, 8; Martin Zabala Xinhua News Agency/Newscom, 11; Sefa Karacan/Anadolu Agency/Getty Images, 13; Romano Cagnoni/Hulton Archive/Getty Images, 14; Jean-Claude Francolon/ Gamma-Rapho via Getty Images, 17; Beth Swanson/Shutterstock.com, 19; Andreas Gradin/Shutterstock.com, 22; Solarseven/Shutterstock.com, 25; FOX SEARCHLIGHT PICTURES/Album/Newscom, 26; MARKET SQUARE PRODUCTIONS/Album/Newscom, 28, 30; AF Archive/Alamy, 33, 43; Pacific Coast News/Newscom, 35; Entertainment Pictures/Entertainment Pictures/ZUMAPRESS.com, 36; Universal History Archive/UIG via Getty images, 40; Ad Media/Splash News/Newscom, 44; Lawrence Lucier/Getty Images, 46; Charles Walker/Topfoto/The Image Works, 48; Gregory MD/ Sciences Source/Getty Images, 54; Science Picture Company/Collection Mix/Getty, 56; Anand Varma/National Geographic/Getty Images, 59.

Printed in the United States of America

CONTENTS

Zombies are members of the undead—said to rise from their graves.

INTRODUCTION

Since the first humans walked the earth, myths and legends have engaged minds and inspired imaginations. Ancient civilizations used stories to explain phenomena in the world around them: the weather, tides, and natural disasters. As different cultures evolved, so too did their stories. From their traditions and observations emerged creatures with powerful abilities, mythical intrigue, and their own origins. Sometimes, different cultures encouraged various manifestations of the same creature. At other times, these creatures and cultures morphed into entirely new beings with greater powers than their predecessors.

Today, societies still celebrate the folklore of their ancestors—on-screen in presentations such as *The Hobbit*, *The Walking Dead*, and *X-Men*; and in stories such as *Harry Potter* and *Twilight*. Some even believe these creatures truly existed and continue to walk the earth as living creatures. Others resign these beings to myth.

In the Creatures of Fantasy series, we celebrate captivating stories of the past from all around the world. Each book focuses on creatures both familiar and unknown: the terrifying ghost, the bloodthirsty vampire, the classic Frankenstein, mischievous goblins, enchanting witches, and the callous zombie. Here their various incarnations throughout history are brought to life. All have their own origins, their own legends, and their own influences on the imagination today. Each story adds a new perspective to the human experience and encourages people to revisit tales of the past in order to understand their presence in the modern age.

THEY WALK AMONG US

"When there's no more room in hell, the dead will walk the earth."

DAWN OF THE DEAD

THEY'RE COMING.

In a big city, the roads have been blocked off and traffic has been diverted. It's almost as though there is an event being held, but the streets are empty. There are no carnival rides, no happy sounds of people enjoying a parade. Instead, there's a chorus of moans coming from thousands of different voices. What is going on?

They come into view. A huge mass of people stumbling awkwardly. They move as a singular group, inching forward as they let out growls and groans. Their legs are stiff and slump along as though they can't quite control their bodies. Some have their arms outstretched for balance. As they come closer, it becomes clear that

Opposite: A man dressed as a zombie is covered in blood.

their clothes are splattered with blood. Was there a disaster? Are these people hurt; do they need help? They inch closer. There is dark blood smeared across their mouths. The groans get louder, more pronounced. They seem to be saying, "Braiiiins!" over and over. Oh no, get out! The zombies are coming!

This terrifying sight can be seen regularly all across the world, especially around Halloween. Why haven't there been tales and news reports of massive zombie attacks and outbreaks? Because this is a zombie walk, of course!

Zombie Walk

Zombie walks have become increasingly popular over the past ten years. They are organized groups of people who get together and dress up as zombies, and then—you guessed it—go for a walk. People get together and put on face paint, ripped clothes, and fake blood to stumble around and portray a mass of the undead who have returned from their graves. Some zombie walks are officially sanctioned and get permits to block off streets, kind of like parades. Others are smaller and less organized, just a few people on the sidewalk or walking through a park. It doesn't take many people to have a zombie walk.

The first recorded zombie walk was held in Sacramento, California, in 2001. Bryna Lovig organized the walk to promote a midnight horror film festival. People came out in their most ghoulish outfits and walked as a group of zombies through the night. It was a success. Ever since, zombie walks have been a fiendishly fun event for horror enthusiasts.

The rash of zombie films that came out a few years later certainly added to this strange craze. In 2005, a remake of the classic zombie movie *Dawn of the Dead* came out, and so did four hundred zombies

This is part of the crowd that showed up for the Buenos Aires zombie walk in 2014.

for a zombie walk in Vancouver, Canada. Eight hundred zombies stepped out in 2006 in Pittsburgh, Pennsylvania, at the Monroeville Mall, where the original *Dawn of the Dead* film had been shot. As years progressed and zombie movies started appearing more frequently at the box office, zombie walks became more popular. Soon cities across the country were holding their own zombie walks, from small get-togethers to huge organized parades of bloody, stumbling ghouls. Grand Rapids, Michigan, had eight thousand people show up in their very best costumes of the living dead and briefly held the Guinness World Record for top zombie turnout.

However, a craze as darkly delightful as this one could not be kept for the United States and Canada alone. The zombie walk quickly spread beyond North America. As of 2012, twenty-three countries had held officially sanctioned zombie walks. There may be even more countries that have held unofficial ones! Some of the largest zombie walks have occurred in South America, where zombies and their hunger for brains have become hugely popular. In 2012 in Santiago, Chile, around twelve thousand people showed up gray-faced and bloody at a zombie walk, only to have their numbers trounced when Buenos Aires had twenty-four thousand "undead" roaming their streets the same year.

The current record holder for most "undead" to show up at a zombie walk is Minneapolis/St. Paul, Minnesota. Around thirty thousand people showed up to their zombie walk in 2012. However, these stats change quickly, and more people seem to fall in love with the idea of being "undead" every day!

Brains for Benefits

Zombie walks are a lot of fun, and many of them are organized as a community for people to dress up and walk around together. However, lots of zombie walks have been organized as fundraisers and benefits for important causes—for food drives, in which hungry zombies bring canned goods and other food as admission for wandering around and pretending to take a bite out of people's brains; and as a part of blood and organ donation fundraisers, a fun, if literal, interpretation of a zombie's hunger for human flesh.

Many zombie tales involve a disease infecting normal people and turning them into zombies. Then the mysterious plague spreads across the world. Some organizers look at this aspect of zombie myth and form their fundraiser around the metaphor of a zombie virus. Zombie walks have raised money for common diseases such as heart disease, colitis, and Crohn's disease. Some with a particularly dark sense of humor have set up zombie walk benefits for people suffering brain trauma and in one particular case, in memory of a man who died from necrotizing fasciitis, the flesh-eating disease.

So what is the appeal? Why have zombies become such a cult phenomenon? It is undeniable that people around the world have fallen in love with zombies. The fad has spread almost as quickly as a true zombie plague. Yet with films, television shows, video games, iPad apps, and truly hilarious zombie-infiltrated literature, where does the zombie myth begin?

Zombie runs are a great way to get adrenaline pumping!

Run, Run, As Fast As You Can

Think a zombie walk is too slow a pace to be much fun? With the rise of zombie popularity, many different types of zombie-organized fun have popped up. The more athletically minded have created apps for smartphones that put runners through a workout avoiding imaginary zombies. The app Zombies, Run! is one such audible storyline, part computer game, part workout, where the phone measures your pace to see whether or not you outrun a fictionalized zombie attack. These apps are full of gross sound effects and scary music to keep a user's heart racing.

For those in search of a more realistic experience, there are zombie runs. An organized zombie run is something like flag football. A participant decides if they want to be a zombie or a human. If he or she decides to be human, they are given three flags to wear around a belt. Then when the race begins, runners go through obstacles and run into large hordes of zombies, who attempt to "infect" them by tearing off these health flags. If a runner loses all three flags, they become infected.

Other less structured games have popped up that pit humans against people playing infected undead. One of the most popular is Humans vs. Zombies, which has numerous variations and can be played with any amount of people. The fight for survival is a popular activity for those who crave "flesh-eating" fun.

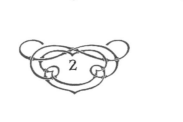

THE HAITIAN ZOMBIE

"People who die and are resurrected ... but without their souls."

Zora Neale Hurston

IT MAY SURPRISE YOU THAT THE ZOMBIE of today is unrecognizable from the zombie of the past. The **zombi**, or Caribbean **voodoo** zombie, was a completely different creature, whose mythology and cultural background is just as fascinating and quite possibly more terrifying than the zombie we know now.

According to legend, the zombi was a normal person who had been transformed into a mindless servant by a witch doctor through dark voodoo magic. This witch doctor would essentially abduct and brainwash his or her victims to do his or her bidding. People would be trapped for years, forced into mindless labor, unable to escape. It was a truly terrifying risk for those who lived

Opposite: A group of men dress up as zombies to perform a Haitian ritual.

where the voodoo religion was prevalent. Voodoo was especially popular in Haiti.

The first American account of the zombi was written by Patrick Lafcadio Hearn. Hearn was a **sensationalist** journalist who travelled the world recording strange stories from far off places. He wrote the first article about zombies for *Harper's Magazine* in 1889, as part of an essay on Caribbean magic and lore. It was called "Country of the Comers Back." He did his best to uncover information about the stories of the "walking dead" in Martinique but found that inhabitants were particularly uncomfortable discussing the tales.

In 1932, Zora Neale Hurston, an anthropologist and famous writer, went to investigate this strange monster that haunted bedtime stories. What she found amazed her. There seemed to be much more truth to the zombi myth than originally thought. She discovered that stories of people rising from the dead and working for an overlord who controlled them—the story of the zombi— could have some basis in fact. When she presented her findings, few took her seriously. In part, this was because the claims seemed outrageous. How could someone rise from the dead? Others believed that the voodoo zombi story was instead a metaphor for slavery—the idea that a person could be captured and forced to do labor against their will was a prevalent theme in Caribbean countries. Haiti, for example, had been controlled by white owners of sugar plantations for generations, and black slave labor powered these plantations.

Clairvius Narcisse: The Living Proof

The discussion of the existence of the zombi was largely ignored until the curious case of Clairvius Narcisse. In 1962, Narcisse had

come into the Albert Schweitzer Hospital with aches and pains. He had critically low blood pressure, hypothermia, and suffered from digestive problems and respiratory failure. Two doctors looked after him, one Haitian, one American.

Ti Femme (*left*) and Clairvius Narcisse (*right*) "returned from the dead." They had been poisoned and forced to become zombies.

Even though he received very good treatment, he died in a few days. His sister identified his body and there was a funeral. He was buried on the day of his death, and ten days later a tombstone was put on his as yet undisturbed grave.

The story of Narcisse is very sad but unremarkable up to this point. It wasn't until many years later that this story became something more. In 1981, nearly twenty years after his death, his sister walked through her local market. She saw a man who looked just like her brother. The man approached her and told her that he was, in fact, her long-dead brother Clairvius. He explained that he had been transformed into a zombi and was forced to work on a sugar plantation until the person controlling him died. Understandably, she didn't believe the news. However, he then called her by the childhood nickname he had for her, something only the two of them would know.

Many disregarded this story as an **urban legend**. However, the intriguing circumstances led to further investigation. Lamarck Douyon, director of the Pyschiatric Institute in Port-au-Prince, was especially interested and decided to research the situation. Was Narcisse just a con artist who was taking advantage of a bereaved family member, or was his story true? Luckily, it was easy for Douyon to investigate. For one thing, the recorded medical records

of the death of Clairvius Narcisse were available. Because Albert Schwietzer Hospital was in part run by medical staff from the United States, the hospital kept very organized records and was considered highly dependable. After reviewing the records, it was clear that a man named Clairvius Narcisse had been determined dead after several days in the hospital and was buried. The next part was harder: to find out if the man who was alive was really Clairvius Narcisse. Since DNA testing had not yet been invented, Douyon had to confirm the man's identity through other means. In order to do that, Douyon sat down with the Narcisse family to construct the ultimate identity test. He asked Clairvius Narcisse question after question about private family matters, nicknames, and events from the past that only the true Narcisse would know. The man answered the questions and passed Douyon's identity test with flying colors. He was the real Narcisse.

Many more began to investigate the voodoo zombi myth after this story came to light. However, for the inhabitants of the Caribbean islands, as well as practitioners of voodoo, the zombi has long been a present and very real fear. In fact, the Criminal Code of the Republic of Haiti once had on its books a law dealing specifically with zombis. According to Article 246, a zombi was a person who had been poisoned by a voodoo priest and put into a "state of lethargy." This stasis made the person appear dead. After the victims were buried, the priest would "resurrect" the person, but as a zombi.

For many years people believed that the individuals they buried were all at risk of being resurrected to this horrible half-life, and families buried their loved ones by busy crossroads or in the back of their houses to try to discourage evil priests from stealing the bodies. However, it became clear that zombies did

Poison extracted from the puffer fish is an important ingredient in the poison that transforms a person into a zombi.

not actually die but were poisoned into a half-life state. Priests could not resurrect someone who had actually died. They could only kidnap those they had poisoned.

Despite the voodoo zombi bearing little resemblance to the zombies that are so popular today, it does have a few things in common with the horror movie monsters. It's slow, tireless, and impervious to pain. It also seems to be unable to access its higher thinking skills and was portrayed as dumb, much like the mindless modern-day zombie. However, all voodoo zombies were forced to comply with a master's wishes, making them mindless servants. They never had any murderous intent unless forced to hurt someone by their masters. Voodoo zombies were the shells of human beings, more robot than flesh-eater. Most importantly, the voodoo zombies were not actually dead, though understandably there was some initial confusion on this point. So where did the myth of this new zombie come from?

Lichs, Vampires, and Other Undead Ancestors

Zombies as we know them have their origins in many other tales of the undead. One of the zombie's most famous forefathers is

Frankenstein's monster, the creature Mary Shelley created in her masterpiece, *Frankenstein; or, The Modern Prometheus*. Constructed out of the dead bodies of others, this creature's malformed brain and horrible treatment it endured led to a dangerous combination of nature and nurture with murderous consequences.

Other undead creatures certainly had an impact on the formation of the zombie in Western imagination. The vampire, with its need to consume human blood, is something like the well-read older brother of the zombie. Both undead, both with a strong desire to consume humans, they serve as **foils** to one another: the vampire, solitary, educated, upper class; and the zombie, **legion**, mindless, and often a metaphor for the oppressed. Another undead monster that preceded the zombie is the lich, a particular kind of ghoul who is very much like the zombie with the exception that it can recognize family and friends after death—though zombie tales vary on this point. In each instance a person is brought back from the dead, often without his or her consent, only to become violent and a danger to others.

Awaking from a Zombi Dream

American journalist William Buehler Seabrook went to Haiti in 1928 and spent much of his time uncovering myths about the zombi. He eventually collected his research into a book over three hundred pages long called *The Magic Island*. Seabrook was by no means an anthropologist like Zora Neale Hurston, and his research is questionable—for example, his book says that the zombies were returned to their graves, which is highly unlikely. However, his work was the first English book entirely devoted to the zombi, and it became a huge influence on how the English-speaking world perceived the voodoo myth.

One story he recounts is that of dead men working in the sugarcane fields of Hasco, a Haitian-American Sugar Company. A man named Ti Joseph brought a group of dazed, slow-moving men to work in the fields. When asked their names the men stared blankly and were unable to say. They were, according to the man who told Seabrook the story, zombies, dead men who had been woken from their graves to work in the fields. Joseph dropped the men off at camp and specified that they were supposed to be given a bland diet with absolutely no salt. Any money they made he took for himself.

Ti's wife, Croyance, felt pity for the poor men and brought them to a local festival, called Croix des Bouquet. She intended to bring them back to the camp with no problems. However, at the festival the men were given a meat stew with salt in it. Suddenly, they awakened from their voodoo stupor. They wandered off into the mountains and found their families. The local bokor, or voodoo priest, was called. He returned the zombies to their graves and then cursed Ti Joseph, who was later beheaded for his crime.

ZOMBIE STRENGTHS AND WEAKNESSES

"I don't know if there's any such thing as a bad zombie. I mean, I love 'em all."

GEORGE ROMERO

IT HAS BEEN ESTABLISHED THAT A ZOMBIE is a creature that is relatively new in the public eye. Not a zombi, not a lich, not a vampire, this creature of fantasy is different from most monsters that haunt Halloween movies. So what makes a zombie a zombie?

POWER IN NUMBERS

Zombies are undead. This means that in most stories and myths, zombies are people who have risen from the dead. However, beyond that they do not seem to have any supernatural powers. They do not hypnotize like the vampire, nor do they transform under a full moon like the werewolf. Most zombies aren't even particularly strong.

Opposite: Zombies are some of the most popular monsters of today—so what are they, really?

Red pupils are a sure sign of a zombie infected with the "rage virus."

Fast Zombies

An important variation on the zombie monster is the fast zombie, who made its most famous appearance in the film *28 Days Later*, only then to show up in the movie version of *World War Z* and video games such as *The Last of Us*. Fast zombies are very different from the typical undead creatures shuffling along the path. For one thing, fast zombies are not dead. There's no decomposing body, no half-decayed flesh hanging from the bones like threads. These are people who have contracted a very specific, very horrible virus.

In the film *28 Days Later*, victims contract the "rage virus": a horrible disease that infects people and fills them with an extremely destructive rage. All rage zombies want to do is kill. Unlike the slow, wandering zombies, these zombies do not hold on to their shreds of humanity. Instead, the infected shed their clothes and embrace the animalistic. These zombies don't groan, but they don't sound human either. The sounds they make are shrieks similar to the fighting screams of wild animals. This makes sense, since in the film the "rage virus" was a disease created in a laboratory in experiments on monkeys.

Fast zombies are much more dangerous than classic zombies. By embracing a wild animal nature, they are faster than uninfected humans, and sometimes stronger. These zombies are fearless, just as the classic zombies, and while there is some debate over whether or not they feel physical discomfort, it is clear that pain, maiming, and death are risks they are more than willing to take if it means killing a human. In some specific instances, fast zombies even take on superhuman powers and are able to jump much higher, and run much faster, than any human possibly could.

If anything, their only superpower is their lack of power. They cannot be deterred by garlic or crosses or silver bullets.

Despite this rather disappointing lack of magical abilities, the zombie does have a few strengths that enable it to dismantle society and create **anarchy**. Firstly, a zombie does not feel pain. Hack off the arm of a zombie and it will still come after you. They feel no discomfort from the cold, they never tire, and they do not sleep. This leads to the second "power" that zombies have: their single-minded goal of slaughter. There is no monster more determined to kill than a zombie. In fact, to attack and to eat human flesh are the only real goals zombies seem to have. They do not care about anything else, and they do not form relationships with one another. The only thing a zombie wants or needs is to kill humans and eat their guts.

A single zombie does not pose much of a threat. Most films, video games, and other zombie representations show human heroes easily overpowering and escaping a lone zombie that happens to find them. However, there is never just one zombie. The zombie represents a plague on humanity. This plague is always highly infectious and usually the only thing supernatural about zombies at all. In some of the original zombie movies from the 1960s, these plagues were said to have come from outer space. Essentially, the dead rise up from their graves or the hospital or the morgue and begin to attack others. Once a person is bitten by a zombie, he or she is infected. It is only a matter of time before the person succumbs to the disease and also becomes a zombie. Because of this, the disease spreads quickly, and within a day there are massive hordes of zombies roaming the streets. This is where zombies get their power: not in the individual monster but in the swarm of

hungry undead. Healthy humans, or the "uninfected," maybe be able to fight off a zombie or two, but when the zombies number fifty or more, the odds become much less favorable.

In all zombie myths, the zombie seems uniquely able to seek out its human prey, despite its poor reasoning skills. This has led some to believe that zombies have a very strong sense of smell. However, their ability to find humans could simply exist because they once were human. It is possible that zombies aren't quite as brain-dead as we expect them to be. In many instances, zombies recognize where humans congregate—a mall, a farmhouse, even a military base. They may not have specific memories of the past or remember who friends and family are, but in many tales zombies have the instinct to mimic humans.

How to Kill a Zombie

There are many different approaches to killing zombies, and it varies depending on the type of zombie that is featured in the

Taking on zombies is no task for the faint of heart.

tale. The fast zombie may die on its own through starvation, but it can also be killed in a variety of ways—essentially, an infected person is still a living person, and a shot to the heart should do it. However, slow, or classic, zombies are extremely difficult to kill. This is because they are already dead. A classic zombie may be cut in two and still pursue its attackers. This is why

Fire is one of the few things that scare zombies.

riddling a slow zombie with bullets is ineffective, as is drowning or strangulation. However, zombies are not as specific as the werewolf, who needs silver, or the vampire, who will die if they are stabbed in the heart with a wooden stake.

The key to a zombie's undead life is its brain. This may have been what contributed to the belief that zombies hunger for brains above all. In truth, the earliest zombies did not care if they were eating guts, arms, legs, or eyeballs. However, damage to the brain stops a zombie. A shot to the head is very effective, but many heroes throughout stories have used bats, pipes, two-by-fours, and other weapons (even, in one particular instance, vinyl records) to bash in the brains of their attackers. This approach can be used with all zombies and is even effective in the case of superhuman fast zombies, who are not bothered by most other attacks, despite their status as technically alive.

A zombie in all forms, slow or fast, animalistic or barely aware, has a few fears that can be used to a human's advantage. Like most monsters from classic Hollywood horror films, zombies are afraid of fire. They shrink away from torches and will avoid heat and light at all costs. There are several theories as to why. In some stories, zombies avoid all light and are afraid of the sun, becoming practically nocturnal. However, most zombies walk about in broad daylight and their twenty-four-hour hunting is what makes them distinctly horrible. In other stories, zombies seem no longer able to understand the concept of fire, and fear it like wild animals. Either way, the most practical reason for this fear could be self-preservation. Like the vampire, zombies are susceptible to fire. Burning a zombie is a relatively easy way to kill it, compared to hand-to-hand combat. Setting up explosions, dowsing zombies with gasoline, and creating **Molotov cocktails** are all easy ways to take out many zombies at once.

However, there is usually a catch to the fast zombie if uninfected humans are able to "wait out the storm," so to speak. These viruses are so overwhelming and change the instincts of humans so much that they forget to nourish themselves. While the classic zombie is obsessed with eating flesh, the fast zombie is merely obsessed with infecting and killing. Because they are alive, they need food to eat, but in several stories, these infected people simply forget. This means that the typical fast zombie outbreak can actually be taken care of by waiting until the zombies starve to death.

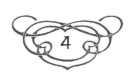

A NIGHT TO REMEMBER

"They're coming to get you, Barbara."

NIGHT OF THE LIVING DEAD

Z OMBIES ARE STILL VERY NEW COMPARED to the monsters that have been around for hundreds and in some cases thousands of years. Because of this, there is no main zombie myth, as such. Perhaps in another hundred years or so we can say that zombies and their stories have endured enough time to become a part of American folklore, or even international myth. However, some stories are more well known than others, and one is the most famous of all.

Night of the Living Dead

When George Romero set out to make a horror film with his independent film company based in Pittsburgh, Pennsylvania, he

Opposite: Zombies from the 1968 film Night of the Living Dead

had no idea that the villains he described in his script would spawn a countercultural phenomenon. He had collected a bunch of friends to make an extremely low-budget film that would take place at an old farmhouse. They spent weeks living in the farmhouse with no running water, each holding multiple roles in production. It became a community project that involved the local police, a butcher, a television news anchor, and a wide variety of volunteers. When they were done, they held a few showings, but it would take a long time before the small film would become a blockbuster success.

Eventually reaching critical acclaim in Europe, the film became part of the horror matinee circuit aimed at children who were used to seeing **campy** tales of horror—such as Vincent Price's reimaginings of Edgar Allen Poe stories. However, its horrific and graphic scenes terrified younger viewers everywhere, and it was quickly realized that the film was more appropriate for the cult scene, with midnight showings popping up around the country.

Night of the Living Dead became a sensation that sparked a whole **genre** of monster horror films that became popular through the 1970s and 1980s, only to return from the grave with increased vigor in the 2010s. However, Romero's hungry undead were not even referred to as zombies in *Night of the Living Dead*. He called them ghouls and said his inspiration did not come from voodoo zombi tales but instead from Richard Matheson's science-fiction classic *I Am Legend*, which features creatures that have become infected with a virus and have been turned into vampires. However, *Night of the Living Dead* laid out the framework and basic plotline for all zombie tales to follow. The story outline below follows the *Night of the Living Dead* framework and those of many other zombie films that have become emblematic of the midnight horror monster.

The Zombie Invasion Begins

It's a quiet, overcast afternoon. People are running errands with their families, maybe to the mall or to the countryside. Perhaps it's a good day to go to the store and buy some snacks in preparation for playing video games. At the beginning of these stories, the **protagonists** notice nothing out of the ordinary, and for the most part, the world around them appears perfectly normal. Everywhere there's a feeling of quiet. A radio show or news program runs a story, but the heroes don't pay attention. Slowly, a person comes toward them. It is possible that the person is just heading toward the same place, the heroes think. They pick up their pace. They realize it is quiet, much too quiet, and that there are no other people around. The person moves in a steady, slow pace and continues to follow the heroes. Finally, annoyed or slightly scared, the heroes confront their pursuer. To their surprise, he or she is silent but attacks, brutally, with the intention to kill. The heroes escape, running quickly away, unaware of what this horrible interaction means.

The heroes of *Shaun of the Dead* stand united after a very long and unusual day.

Every zombie story starts with a normal day that quickly turns into an interaction with someone who appears to be a crazed killer. What the main characters believe is a single disturbed person is actually a zombie coming to kill them. However, what makes a zombie story truly terrifying is the lack of information the characters have about this new situation. No one knows that this is a zombie plague; no one knows what zombies are. The protagonists do not know what is happening, and this puts them in a dangerous position.

In many instances, the first instincts of the main characters are to call the police about the person who attacked them, only to find that the phone line is busy and they are unable to get through. They turn on the television or the radio and hear that this is happening around the region: that the police are overwhelmed with calls reporting violent attackers; that people are being bitten; and that instructions from government officials say to stay away from strangers and stay home or try to get to shelters, hospitals, and other community gathering points for safety.

A Plan Is Formed

At this point, the main characters develop a plan for dealing with this strange invasion of violent infected people. They form a group, usually somewhat out of coincidence, with other people— sometimes it's neighbors, friends, or relatives; often it's just other survivors who think that they will have a better chance of surviving if they stick together. Whatever the relationship, family, friend, or stranger, the group comes up with a plan of surviving.

What makes most zombie narratives so compelling is not the diseased monsters but the interactions of the people who aren't infected. These people are often a diverse group, either by race,

Zombie myths
often start with
widespread panic.

Ben, the main character of *Night of the Living Dead*, hits another character, a white man. This was unheard of in Hollywood at the time.

Unlikely Heroes

Film theorist Robin Wood has said, "Horror film has consistently been one of the most popular and, at the same time, **disreputable** of Hollywood genres." Zombies, werewolves, and vampires may send chills across a silver screen, but rarely do people look for a deeper meaning or positive message when they decide to pay for a ticket to a scary film. Because of this, horror, and specifically the zombie genre, has been able to make some of the most radical statements in Hollywood.

It is often difficult to know who the hero of a zombie narrative is. Generally, audiences are led to believe that strong, handsome men are the heroes, as is often the way in adventure stories. However, zombie movies have a long history with the oppressed. The first film to ever cast a person of color in a role that was not written specifically for a minority was *Night of the Living Dead*. In the film, we think that Barbara, the attractive blonde, will be the star with her handsome brother, Tom. However, it turns out that the narrative actually focuses around Ben, played by Duane Jones, a black man. While this may seem normal now, it was a tremendous step forward in the 1960s. Similarly, in *28 Days Later*, we think that the army will lead everyone to safety and heroics, but it is up to the Irishman Jim to save the day, a very strange event in a British film. Even in the recent video game *The Last of Us*, players assume that the main character is a man named Joel, but it may just be the little girl he's supposed to be protecting.

Zombies and the media they are in have taken a hallowed place in the horror genre as political **allegory**. These stories display how the real world would crack under the right pressure. The destruction and anarchy the stories portray allow viewers, players, and readers to experience a social order that is outside the norm. By watching this new social order—little girls in charge, or black men as heroes—the audience examines their assumptions about the real world.

country, economic status, sex, gender, or age. As society crumbles around them, they have to decide who is in charge. This can often lead to disagreements. There are power struggles between different people who want to be in charge, and often this leads to a viscous dictatorship—what one leader says goes. Many times, this setup allows people who wouldn't otherwise be in charge according to the traditional rules of society to lead. Many zombie movies have been considered politically radical for enabling characters who are usually relegated to bit parts to become something more.

The group has to work together, but there are **schisms** between the people who all ultimately know that death is a very real possibility. They become, as far as they know, the last humans in their area, unable to reach anyone from the outside world. Phones don't work. Radios seem to be useless. All the group can do is wait out the zombies and hope they aren't killed before an outside force can rescue them. In some narratives, this means holing up in a house, barring the doors and windows, and setting traps so that they are protected from the horde of undead. For others, it means a journey to safety, whether that means braving the countryside and being exposed to groups of undead or simply making a trip across town. As the group tries to acquire and pile together their resources, food, water, and weapons become priorities. They end up risking life and limb for access to fresh water, safer corners of the house, or first aid supplies.

Betrayal

Essentially the group works together, but because there is so little trust between members and so much stress on each person, constantly fighting for survival, the group is doomed to fail. Sometimes this is because of a lack of understanding of the

disease. In many films, a person is bitten by a zombie, but because he or she simply doesn't know what is happening, the bitten person stays with the group. The person is even protected by the others, who don't know that a single zombie bite will kill and then turn a normal person into a cannibalistic monster. Other times the person doesn't reveal the bite and, in deep denial, refuses to believe what is happening to him or herself. In any case, this bitten person eventually dies of the bite and then is turned into a horrible monster.

Once this happens, chaos ensues. In some tales, this is because the group has barricaded themselves from the outside world to keep the monsters out, only to be trapped inside with the very thing they wanted to get away from. In others, this simply adds to the chaos of survival and serves as a distraction that ruins the very carefully constructed calm the group needed to function. In many cases, both instances are true. The carefully constructed social dynamic of the group disintegrates as they deal with attacks from all sides.

There are many different endings to zombie tales, and no two are exactly alike. Some are happy; some are extremely pessimistic. Some are ridiculous and funny, while others are strange and gross. In some cases, the zombie plague never goes away. What matters most, though, is that the story of the group of survivors is resolved. Ultimately, even though zombies are the catalysts for all the events, it is the ragtag group of uninfected humans who are the focus of the tale.

When there's no more room in HELL the dead will walk the EARTH

First there was 'NIGHT OF THE LIVING DEAD'

Now

GEORGE A. ROMERO'S

DAWN OF THE DEAD

THE CULT PHENOMENON THAT CANNOT DIE

"Brains for dinner / Brains for lunch
Brains for breakfast / Brains for brunch
Brains at every single meal,
Why can't we have some guts?"
"Braineaters," *Walk Among Us*, The Misfits

BEFORE *NIGHT OF THE LIVING DEAD*, zombies were treated as brainless creatures who would do the bidding of whoever controlled them. After *Night*, however, zombies took on an entirely new dimension: cannibalistic, violent, and without someone controlling them. Zombies became a new but essential and popular monster of horror. In a world of zombies, filling up a tank of gas could become a life-or-death situation, and survival could depend on whether or not there's a baseball bat within reach. Any problem is much more interesting when a group of violent, hungry zombies can swarm and attack.

After George Romero's success with *Night of the Living Dead*, spin-offs and sequels abounded. Zombies became a sensation that spread

Opposite: One of the many zombie installments directed by the father of zombies himself: George Romero.

from film to music to comic books and video games. Romero created five sequels himself: *Dawn of the Dead* had heroes trapped in a mall; *Day of the Dead* focused on research and the military; *Land of the Dead* criticized class structure; *Diary of the Dead* was a return look to group dynamics; and *Survival of the Dead* followed the story of two feuding families dealing with a zombie outbreak. However, with no supernatural powers, no particular intelligence, and no real grounding in magic at all, it may seem amazing that such violent but simple monsters have lit up so many midnight horror movie screens.

HORRALITY

As creepy as zombies are, with their dead eyes, low moan, and constant hunger, there's also something uniquely funny about them. It may be how single-minded they are, or how slow their movements can be, but without a doubt zombies have a certain quirky charm and have become the subject of many horror comedies. There's also the fact that many early zombie films started out with very small budgets. This led to subpar acting, gross but poorly made special effects, and occasionally, bad writing. The high drama that is created by a zombie plot combined with the low quality of the films came together as camp. Camp is a term used to describe something that is so outrageous or absurd that it can't be scary anymore because it is too unrealistic. Instead of being terrifying, a zombie invasion becomes funny. Directors of zombie movies embraced camp and started to use it to their advantage. Soon a whole subset of funny zombie movies started coming out.

Dubbed as "horrality," a mix of hilarity and horror, this group of zombie films uses the same device as horror films—a swarm of mindless undead—to make people laugh. Often these films

are full of slapstick or physical humor gags involving undead violence and funny ways of killing zombies. Heads don't just get hit, they explode. *Shaun of the Dead* (2004), one of the most famous horror-comedies, has a scene in which heroes attack a zombie in a choreographed dance battle. In some films, zombies even get brought into the culture, becoming very much like a serving class—a biting indictment of the class system and the mistreatment of the poorer class. Sometimes zombies even appear as pets, as in the horror-comedy *Fido*, in which a boy has a pet zombie. In these comedies, when a hero dies, they don't just die, but take several minutes of labored breathing to poorly act out a totally unbelievable death.

Camp and horrality give viewers a fun **romp** of slapstick violence and dark humor, with plenty of winks to the audience. There are references to other more serious horror films, and even the occasional political satire. Horrality films open up the zombie genre to a world beyond horror-movie enthusiasts, making the zombie more comedic and mainstream.

Edgar Wright's *Shaun of the Dead* featured some inventive zombie deaths, including execution by vinyl record.

Undead Rock Stars

Camp and violence were the perfect mixture to make the zombie craze irresistible to the punk rock movement and what was eventually known as the **psychobilly rock** of the 1970s and 1980s. The Misfits, with their debut punk album *Walk Among Us*, released

Members of the Misfits pose for a picture at the Rock and Roll Hall of Fame.

a variety of songs, such as "Skulls," "Braineaters," and "Astro Zombies," in which the band sings of being turned into monstrous beings, including zombies and aliens. The lyrics were of wanting to kill, being bored with eating brains, and exterminating the human race. While this reached a specific audience, zombies went mainstream in a big way with Michael Jackson's song "Thriller," complete with a fourteen-minute music video.

Video Games

Zombies seemed tailor-made to be the perfect opponents in a video game. Deadly but dumb, they attacked wildly and seemed to be in endless supply. Unsurprisingly, zombie video games became incredibly popular. The first-ever zombie video game, *Zombie Zombie*, was put out by Quicksilva for ZX Spectrum as early as 1984. Since then, a host of successful games have come out featuring zombies of every possible variation: fast, slow, dumb, smart, from easy cannon fodder to nearly impossible-to-kill bosses.

Zombies have been featured in every type of video game as well, from the first- and third-person shooters such as *Left 4 Dead* and *The Last of Us* to puzzle and role-playing games (RPGs) such as the original 1996 *Resident Evil*. There was even a *Typing of the Dead* game, a typing tutor that was produced as part of the House of the Dead series. Some zombie video games today are marketed as extremely violent or terrifying, such as *Half-Life* and *Left 4 Dead*, while others are more family friendly, such as *Plants vs. Zombies*.

The Zombie in Print

Interestingly, the zombie is the first monster not to have been a part of literature but to originate on film. However, since their introduction, there has been a flourish of zombie books available for the eager reader. Zombie books span the gamut of zombie genres, from terrifying zombie tales to farce. The book *The Zombie Survival Guide* (2003), intended as a farce on survival guides, became a huge hit and was taken just a bit too literally by many. Seth Grahame-Smith made a splash in the literary scene when he released *Pride and Prejudice and Zombies* (2009), a gruesome if hilarious reinterpretation of Jane Austen's *Pride and Prejudice* (1813), in which he inserted zombies into the famous text. Not only are zombies popular **pulp** but a cult favorite in comics, taking center stage in the *Marvel Zombies* series, in *Deadworld*, and even in a manga called *High School of the Dead*.

Resident Evil

When thinking of a good zombie game, it is impossible not to come up with one of the many *Resident Evil* video games that have come out over the past twenty years. The first *Resident Evil* debuted in 1996. It was a third-person shooter but incorporated puzzles and role-playing game aspects. Characters Jill Valentine and Chris Redfield explore a mansion that is infested with zombies as they try to find out what happened to their compatriots and contain the outbreak.

After its initial success, the company Capcom followed up with sequel after sequel, experimenting with the form of the game but always having humans killing off hordes of undead. *Resident Evil* has become one of the most successful and critically praised video game franchises, with more than twenty games of human-versus-zombie gore.

The success of the series lent itself to other genres: novels, comic books, and movies. The first film, *Resident Evil*, came out in 2002. While the film received poor ratings from critics, it did very well with horror enthusiasts, and four other live-action films have been released. Two animated, or CG, films have also been released following a different story line. There seems to be no stopping the *Resident Evil* craze, as a sixth film in the series, *Resident Evil: The Final Chapter*, is set to be released in September 2016.

Opposite: Resident Evil, Code: Veronica was released in 2002.

Yog-Sothoth
Knows the gate
Yog-Soth... gate
Y...

That is not
which can etern
And with strar
even death may

H.P. Lovecraft
1890 = 1937

GRUESOME TALES OF THE UNDEAD

*"Not only is it creepy but it just seems like it's unrelenting—
he's not going to stop."*

GALE ANNE HURD, PRODUCER OF *THE WALKING DEAD*

THE ZOMBIE IS A NEW PHENOMENON, but that doesn't mean that the living dead first came around in the twentieth century, nor is the idea of waking the dead to serve a master exclusive to the voodoo religion. Cultures around the world have talked about beings rising from their graves for centuries.

A DUNWICH HORROR

H. P. Lovecraft, one of the most terrifying writers, is considered among the first authors of science fiction. Set in small New England towns, his horror stories were often gothic and creepy, subtly hinting

Opposite: H. P. Lovecraft with some of his most famous monsters

that there was something not quite right. On the other hand, his horrifying monsters could lead to some truly gruesome ends.

Lovecraft created his own kind of zombie in 1922, when the only zombie known was the voodoo zombie from Haiti. He wrote a **serialized** short story series for the **amateur** journal *Home Brew*. "Herbert West: Reanimator," would become known as one of the zombie predecessors and would later inspire Italian **slasher** zombie movies of the 1980s. The story ran for six issues and followed Herbert West, a medical student who worked on reanimating the dead. In the tale, West creates a **serum** that can bring corpses back to life, and when typhoid fever—a very real plague—hits the small town, he uses his new serum to bring back and "save" whom he can. But the life he brings them back to is not the life they had. To quote a horror movie trope, "They came back … wrong." These reanimated corpses are extremely violent, animalistic, and homicidal. However, the true monster of the tale is Herbert West, who resorts to murder to get new specimens for his experiments.

Unlike the typical zombies, they can communicate, form plans, and seem to have a supernatural connection to each other. They band together to take revenge on West, who gets his just desserts in a horrific nightmare of justice.

The Hopping Dead

A much older tale of violent undead creatures comes from the East. The Chinese *chiang-shih*, which translated is "hopping corpse," is an undead being that is something between a vampire and a zombie. A chiang-shih is a monster that comes back from the dead because its soul cannot ascend to heaven—possibly because of a suicide or an execution. Unlike zombies, they do have supernatural abilities,

and with them, supernatural weaknesses. However, like the zombie, once a chiang-shih comes back from the dead, it no longer has any semblance of a personality.

The monster is known by its greenish skin and long, sharp fingernails. Its mouth is full of elongated, serrated teeth and a pointed tongue. And, much like a slow zombie, a new chiang-shih walks stiffly and limps, as though the body is still feeling the effects of **rigor mortis**. Because of this, they hop after their victims, unable to run, which is what earned them their name. The favorite targets of these creatures are pretty women, who they try to ravage.

Chiang-shihs become stronger and smarter with age and eventually can become extremely powerful, able to shape-shift and possess supernatural strength. Taoist priests with special protection and training are the only ones said to be able to face such powerful monsters. However, initially the chiang-shih is quite weak, and fighting a new chiang-shih is significantly easier than killing a zombie. It is said that the youngest can even be fought off with a broom.

The easiest way to avoid a chiang-shih is to cross a bridge, as they cannot cross moving water. The chiang-shihs are very skittish as well, and banging a pan or making a loud noise reminds them of thunder, which they fear—supposedly because a lightning strike is one of the few ways a chiang-shih can truly die. While shooting a chiang-shih with a bullet will put it down, the creature will rise again unless it is swiftly cremated.

The Dreaded Draugar

Another ancient tale from Norse mythology talks of beings that escaped from their tombs. The *Draugar* were sometimes described as people who had been lost at sea, resurrected after washing up on

shore. Others were described as having died and been buried, only to rise from their graves as smoke.

The Draugar are often depicted as having seaweed in their hair, a nod to the fact that they were probably drowned. Their flesh was pale, usually white, black, or sometimes green. One thing was consistent: the horrible smell of rotting flesh and seawater. These undead were more like ghosts than traditional zombies and were able to change their physical size to be as tall as giants.

Once a Draugr (singular of Draugar) escaped from its grave, it was intent on causing mayhem and violence. Often the Draugar would grow to enormous size and crush their victims. In some tales, their tactics were much more zombie-like: they would attack by biting flesh and consuming their victims. Though these Norse tales vary, there is much evidence that the Draugar were believed to eat their victims' body parts and drink their blood.

Unfortunately, these undead were nearly impossible to re-kill. Only heroes from Norse myths were known to survive and fight the Draugar. Often it was the Norse gods themselves who had to stop the Draugar's murderous rampages. Because of this, Norse people did everything they could to ensure that the people they buried would not rise up. Burial traditions included stabbing iron scissors into the chest of the dead or ramming needles through the soles of the feet so that they could not walk. At the very least, the feet would be tied together. The Norse also tried to confuse the corpse by turning a coffin in different directions, hoping this would prevent a Draugr from getting out. In extreme cases, the door of the burial tomb would be walled with bricks. All this was done so that the undead could not escape their tombs.

Baykok, the Undead Hunter

The Ojibwe tribe of the Great Lakes region, also known as the Chippewa, have their own tales of an undead cannibal who hunts in the night. According to legend, the *baykok*, which roughly translated means "skin-draped bones," was once a fierce and talented hunter determined to get his prey. One day, he saw a large buck in the forest, a prize for any hunter. He shot at it but missed. Rather than give up, he followed the deer. Again he shot at it and again the animal moved away just in time. In his pride, the baykok followed the buck for days. Tired and hungry, he continued his journey until he lay on the ground too weak to move, dying of starvation. He was so incredibly hungry—but he was also furious. How could the deer have evaded him so well? With his dying breath, he refused to give up his hunt, swearing that his soul would never leave his body. Then, he died.

A while after his death, a group of hunters came across his body, which was decayed and mostly bones. His spirit was disturbed by the hunters, and he awoke, his soul still inhabiting his dead body. **Ravenous**, he shot up and brutally murdered the small group, feasting on their bodies. However, he was not satisfied. Forever hungry, even in death, the baykok stalks the night, preying on lone hunters and warriors who come across his path. He is armed with a quiver of invisible spirit arrows and a mighty club.

A ZOMBIE APOCALYPSE IN OUR FUTURE?

"Poverty, unemployment, overpopulation, disease, rioting;
all crucial elements in creating a nightmare zombie wasteland."

JOSS WHEDON

A NEWER VERSION OF THE ZOMBIE tale is one that starts after the zombies have taken over. These narratives start after the worst has already happened. The heroes live in a wasteland; the government has been destroyed; and the zombies have taken over the world, getting rid of any kind of organized society. Humanity is left to fend for itself. People live not in large cities but in small villages surrounded by booby traps and high walls. Guns are everywhere. People are violent, and anarchy reigns. It is a time of the survival of the fittest, and each person is ultimately looking out for him or herself.

These tales often follow a plotline of people who are trying to figure out what to do now that society no longer exists. This is a

Opposite: The body of an ant that has been attacked by a parasite, transforming it into a zombie.

common plot for television shows such as *The Walking Dead* (based on the comic of the same name) and *Z Nation*, as it is a longer, more complex tale than most movies generally adopt. In some cases, these long stories have "holy grail" plotlines. A holy grail plotline refers to the tale of King Arthur and his quest for the Holy Grail. It is when people go on a quest for something that may or may not exist. In zombie media, the sought-after item is often a cure for the zombie disease. *Z Nation* and the video game *The Last of Us* both follow this plotline, holding out hope in a world that seems to have none left. However, the question remains: Is a zombie **apocalypse** even possible?

Super Rabies

It has been suggested that rabies could mutate to become a virus

A close-up of the rabies virus

that acts much like the zombie infection, turning human into something similar to Danny Boyle's fast zombies in *28 Days Later*. Rabies may at first glance seem like the logical candidate for mutating into a zombie virus. This is because rabies is often spread by bites, a signature way of spreading disease in zombie films. After a person is bitten by something with rabies— usually animals such as bats or dogs are the culprits— the virus enters through the muscle, then travels to the brain and attacks the nervous system. If rabies goes unchecked, a person can become violent but quickly goes into a coma, which is followed by death.

While it is tempting to think that a zombie apocalypse may be around the corner when a disease like this is around, science says no. For one thing,

rabies takes about one to three months to really cause damage, much too slow to start a zombie apocalypse. Secondly, the rabies virus is not very contagious. It cannot be easily passed from person to person, like the common cold. The virus would have to significantly change in many ways before it could become a likely candidate for a zombie-like disease. It would have to incubate in a matter of hours and become extremely contagious. The likelihood of this happening is nearly impossible. Scientists believe it is safe to say that we never have to fear a zombie virus mutating from rabies.

It Came From Space

Many zombie films use space as the origin of the zombie virus, particularly radiation or some other strange event. This was a common culprit during the movies of the 1960s and 1970s, during the height of the space race. However, some scientists believe that if a zombie virus ever happens, space might very well be the culprit.

There have been several NASA experiments dealing with bacteria and infectious diseases. In one experiment, space flights acted as incubators for *Salmonella* and other bacteria to see how the different environment affected the bacteria. What scientists found is amazing. *Salmonella* became much more deadly after it was flown up in a spaceship and returned home to Earth. Nine out of ten mice died after being infected with the space-incubated *Salmonella*, as opposed to six out of ten mice exposed to the original strain. There is also evidence that the bacteria becomes more **virulent**, meaning that it spreads more quickly as well as being more deadly. This in itself is quite scary, but then it appears that immune systems are less effective in space, meaning that humans would be more susceptible to disease. Finally, there are many viruses that express latent traits when in

space—traits that they always had but had never been activated. Some of these latent traits could prove to be deadly.

Space is a place where bacteria becomes more dangerous, viruses change what they do, and humans are less able to fight off disease. Sounds like the perfect, or rather terrifying, beginning to a zombie outbreak.

Tiny Zombie Overlords

Zombie outbreaks are popular not only in science fiction and horror genres but also in the US government. The Centers for Disease Control and Prevention (CDC) recognize that the quick spread of a zombie outbreak has many similarities to real disease outbreaks. They have even developed a plan of how to contain an actual zombie outbreak if a zombie virus ever was produced—first as a joke, and then as a serious way to encourage engagement and awareness. The Zombie Outbreak Preparedness plan details the best solutions for dealing with zombies, and even includes geographical locations that are most likely to survive.

There is also a "zombification" process that occurs in nature. In these cases, an animal plays **host** to a **parasite**. The parasite takes control of the host animal and forces it to do its bidding. This happens most clearly with insects. Take the *Hymenoepimecis argyraphaga* wasp, for example. It attacks another insect from a specific species, such as the orb spider, and injects it with eggs. The wasp larva then slowly eats the spider from within, and injects its host with a specific chemical. This chemical acts as a mind-control agent and forces the spider to build a strange web—something that it would never have created on its own. Then, the larva kills the host and uses the web to support its cocoon during the pupa stage.

There are many instances of parasites and other organisms controlling their host's behavior for their benefit. In South America, there are a few types of fungi that infect ants. The actions of these infested ants could easily be considered the actions of infected zombies. For the ants' hills, a mini zombie apocalypse is created. The basics are these: an ant is infected with the zombie fungus—of which we know there are at least four different types. This fungus then goes to the ant's brain and takes control of motor functions, forcing the ant to do its bidding.

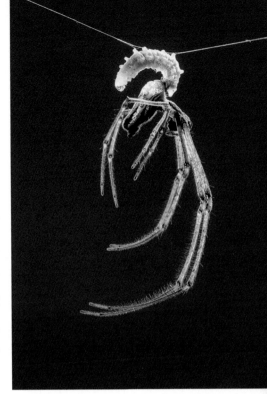

A spider doomed to be a zombie nursery for a wasp

The primary goal of the fungus is to produce as many spores as possible. Often, this means infecting many other ants. For example, a fungus will infect an ant, which then climbs to the top of a blade of grass, usually very close to, if not hanging over, the ant colony or a path that the ants use. It then grows a stalk out of the back of its head, which releases spores on the other ants below, spreading throughout the colony. The zombie virus of *The Last of Us* was based on this fungus, and it shows how truly terrifying such a fungus would be if it spread to humans.

Ultimately, the zombie is a horrific monster, and the implications it brings for epidemics and anarchy are truly terrifying. However, its comic appeal and primetime violence has inspired a love affair with zombies that has spread like an infection throughout popular culture. As long as zombies remain figments of fiction, they will be enjoyed, an essential creature of the monster family.

GLOSSARY

allegory A story in which fictional characters work out symbolic actions to get at a greater truth.

amateur Not professional, lacking experience, or those who participate as a pastime or hobby.

anarchy A state of lawlessness and absence of government.

apocalypse A disaster that causes much destruction, often likened to or sometimes actually the end of the world.

campy Describing something exaggerated or outrageously artificial that fuses with popular culture, often funny.

disreputable Not respectable, untrustworthy.

foil A character that shows traits in contrast with another.

genre A particular type of art or literature.

host An animal in which a parasite lives.

legion Many in number.

Molotov cocktail A crude bomb made out of a bottle filled with flammable liquid that is lit on fire and thrown.

parasite An animal or plant that lives in or on another plant or animal.

protagonist The main character in a story.

psychobilly rock A genre of music that mixes rock, punk, and rockabilly; known for lyrics which reference science fiction, horror, and violence.

pulp Term referring to cheap paper books, often with sensationalist storytelling.

ravenous Extremely hungry.

rigor mortis A temporary stiffness of the body that happens soon after death.

romp An enjoyable or lively experience.

schism A division of a group that occurs when members disagree with one another.

sensationalist Arousing quick emotional reactions or curiosity.

serialized Published in separate parts over a period of time.

serum A fluid that is often blood from another animal that can be added to human blood to cure disease.

slasher A movie in which many people are killed, especially with sharp knives; usually quite gory.

urban legend A story or tall tale that usually takes place in a city, but is outrageous and impossible to source.

virulent Extremely dangerous and spreading very quickly.

voodoo A religion derived from African polytheism and ancestor worship that is practiced primarily in Haiti.

zombi A person controlled by a voodoo witch doctor after being poisoned.

To Learn More About Zombies

Books

Brooks, Max. *The Zombie Survival Guide: Complete Protection from the Living Dead.* New York: Three Rivers Press, 2003.

Curran, Bob. *Zombies, A Field Guide to the Walking Dead.* Franklin Lakes, NJ: Career Press, 2009.

Montandon, Mac. *The Proper Care and Feeding of Zombies.* Hoboken, NJ: Wiley, 2010.

Website

The Zombie Research Society

zombieresearchsociety.com

Everything you want to know about zombies, from the science behind cannibalism to surviving a zombie apocalypse to new films coming out.

Video

Birth of the Living Dead. Directed by Rob Kuhns. Glass Eye Pix. 2013.

Bibliography

Ahlvers, Alicia. "Zombie Walk." In *Encyclopedia of the Zombie: The Walking Dead in Popular Culture and Myth*, edited by Anthony J. Fonseca and June Michele Pulliam, 318–320. Santa Barbara, CA: Greenwood, 2014.

Bates, Mary. "Meet 5 'Zombie' Parasites That Mind-Control Their Hosts." *National Geographic*, November 2, 2014. Accessed July 18, 2015. http://news.nationalgeographic.com/news/2014/10/141031-zombies-parasites-animals-science-halloween.

Boyle, Danny. *28 Days Later*. DVD. Los Angeles: Fox Searchlight, 2003.

Brown, Nathan Robert. *The Complete Idiot's Guide to Zombies*. New York: Alpha, 2010.

Castro, Joseph. "Zombie Fungus Enslaves Only Its Favorite Ant Brains." *Live Science*, September 9, 2014. Accessed July 18, 2015. http://www.livescience.com/47751-zombie-fungus-picky-about-ant-brains.html.

Kaplan, Matt. "Photos: 'Zombie' Ants Found With New Mind-Control Fungi." *National Geographic*, March 5, 2011. Accessed July 19, 2015. http://news.nationalgeographic.com/news/2011/03/pictures/110303-zombie-ants-fungus-new-species-fungi-bugs-science-brazil.

Kuhns, Rob. *Birth of the Living Dead*. DVD. New York: First Run Features, 2014.

McIntosh, Shawn. "The Evolution of the Zombie: The Monster That Keeps Coming Back." In *Zombie Culture: Autopsies of the Living Dead*, edited by Shawn McIntosh and Marc Leverette, 1-17. Lanham, MD: Scarcrow Press, 2008.

Misfits, The. *Walk Among Us*. CD. New York: Rhino Entertainment, 2000.

National Geographic. *National Geographic Classics: Witches, Ghosts, and Monsters*. DVD. Washington, DC: National Geographic Video, 2014.

Resident Evil: The Final Chapter. Accessed July 18, 2015. http://www.imdb.com/title/tt2592614/?ref_=nv_sr_2.

Romero, George. *Night of the Living Dead*. DVD. American Pop Classics, 2012.

Turi, Tim. "Ranking The Entire Resident Evil Series." *Game Informer*, October 27, 2014. Accessed July 11, 2015. http://www.gameinformer.com/b/features/archive/2014/10/27/ranking-the-entire-resident-evil-series.aspx.

Vuckovic, Jovanka. *Zombies!: An Illustrated History of the Undead*. New York: St. Martin's Griffin, 2011.

Index

Page numbers in **boldface** are illustrations. Entries in **boldface** are glossary terms.

About the Author

Amy Hayes studied creative writing, film studies, and children's literature at the University of Pittsburgh. Her first encounter with zombies was a Halloween showing of *Night of the Living Dead* when she was thirteen. It gave her nightmares for years. As such, she has spent a lot of time reading everything about zombies. If she were going to dress up as a zombie, she would most definitely be a dead Vanna White. She spent several years living in Pittsburgh, Pennsylvania, the unofficial zombie capital of the world. She now lives in the beautiful city of Buffalo, New York, a town that is arguably much safer from a zombie apocalypse.